Phonics
Wipe-Clean
Activity Book

for ages 3-5

This CGP wipe-clean book is full of colourful phonics activities for Pre-School and Reception children.

It's a fun way to introduce the essential skills — and you can wipe it clean to enjoy again and again!

Hints for Helpers

Here are a few useful things to know when using this book:

- Your child can use the pen provided to write or draw their answers. They can use their right or left hand — whichever they find easier. The pen can be wiped away when they've finished to allow multiple chances to practise.

- Keep the pen away from your child's eyes. Avoid getting the ink on clothing, furniture or fabric as it may not be washable.

- This book covers Phase Two, and some of Phase Three, of most phonics programmes used in schools, which is often introduced to children at Pre-school, and is also taught in Reception.

- The book helps children to practise some of the most common sounds in the English language and recognise the letters that are usually used to write these sounds.

- This book is designed to be worked through in order. However, the 'Stepping Stones' activity in the centre uses letters from the whole book. You may want to complete this activity last.

- Learning to listen carefully is an important part of learning Phonics. Children should be encouraged to say aloud what they think a picture is, and to listen to the sounds that they make as they say the word. This is great practice, even if they're not ready to start reading for themselves yet.

- Once your child is beginning to tackle reading whole words, encourage them to segment each word into individual sounds, then blend the sounds together to read the whole word.

- For example, to read the word 'sun', they should segment the word into separate sounds — 's', 'u' and 'n', which sound like 'ss', 'u' and 'nn'.

- For each letter, there is a dot showing where to start and arrows to follow to complete the letter.

- Bear in mind that every nursery or school has its own handwriting style. Some schools may form letters differently to how they're written here — for example, k instead of k.

Contents

s, a, t & p	2
i, n, m & d	4
o, g, c & k	6
ck, e & u	8
Stepping Stones	10
r, h & b	12
f, ff, l, ll & ss	14
j, v, w & x	16
qu, y, z & zz	18
Word practice	20

Published by CGP

Editors: Andy Cashmore, Heather Cowley, Hayley Shaw

With thanks to Rebecca Greaves and Gareth Mitchell for the proofreading.

With thanks to Alice Dent for the copyright research.

ISBN: 978 1 78908 975 2

Printed by Elanders Ltd, Newcastle upon Tyne.

Graphics used on the cover and throughout the book © Educlips
Cover design concept by emc design ltd.

Text, design, layout and original illustrations © Coordination Group Publications Ltd. (CGP) 2023
All rights reserved.

CGP, Broughton House, Griffin Street, Broughton-in-Furness, Cumbria, LA20 6HH

CGP c/o Elanders GmbH, Anton-Schmidt-Str. 15, 71332 Waiblingen, GERMANY

Photocopying this book is not permitted, even if you have a CLA licence.
Extra copies are available from CGP with next day delivery • 0800 1712 712 • www.cgpbooks.co.uk

s, a, t & p

First Try This

Trace the letters below with your pen by following the arrows. Say the sounds out loud as you write them.

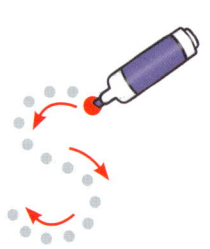 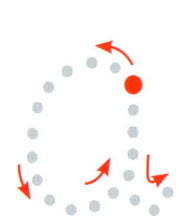 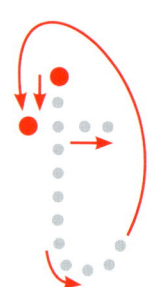 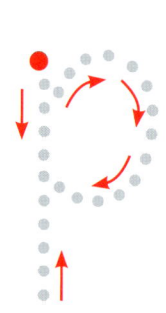

Now Try These

Put a tick under the picture that starts with the **s** sound.

Circle the picture that starts with the **p** sound.

  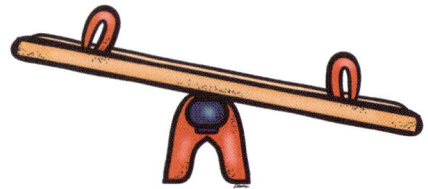

What sound do all these words start with? Trace the right answer.

What is Zara wearing on her head?
Say the word. Trace the letter of the sound you can hear.

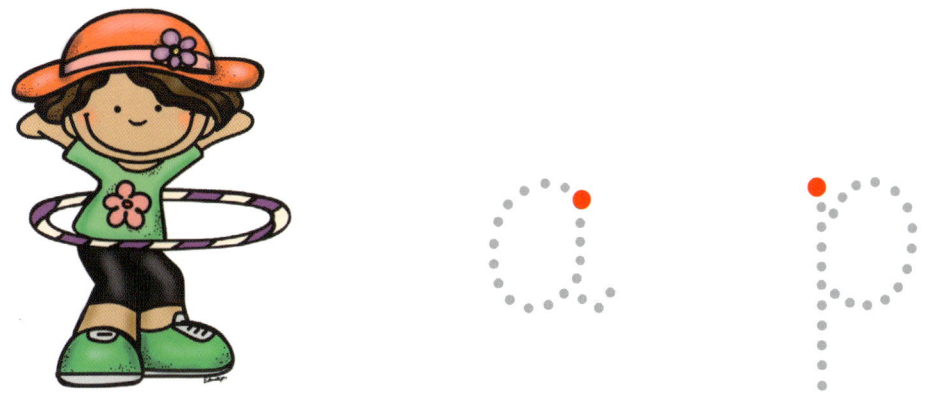

Circle two things on the picnic table that start with the **t** sound.

Great work — you've done a fantastic job! Draw a smiley face.

i, n, m & d

First Try This

Follow the arrows with your pen to trace the letters below.
Say the sounds out loud as you write them.

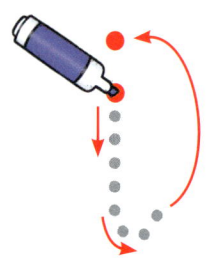 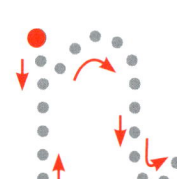 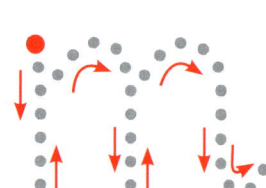 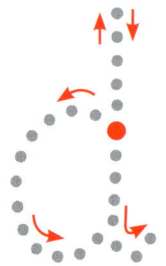

Now Try These

Circle one thing in the picture that starts with the **d** sound.

What are the pictures below? Say each word out loud.
Put a tick under the picture that contains the **i** sound.

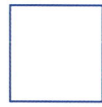  

Circle the picture that starts with the **m** sound.

What part of the dog is the arrow pointing to?
Say the word. Trace the letter of the sound it starts with.

    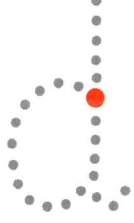

Draw lines to match each picture to the sound it starts with.
Then trace each letter.

Wow, you did paw-some on that page! Draw a smiley face.

5

o, g, c & k

First Try This

Trace the letters below with your pen by following the arrows.
Say the sounds as you write them.

> **c** and **k** make the same sound.

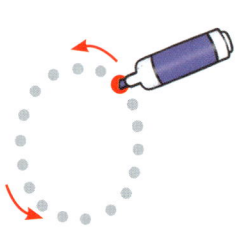 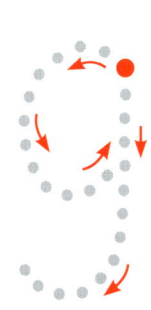 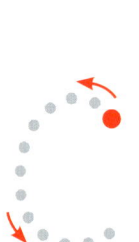 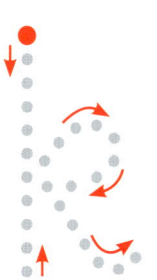

Now Try These

Put a tick under the picture that starts with the **k** sound.

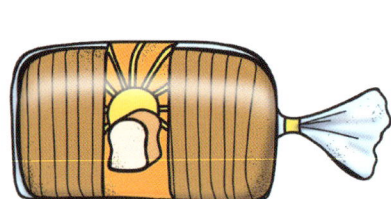      

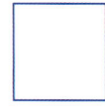      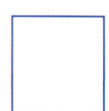

Trace the letters below.
Then circle the sound at the start of all three words.

      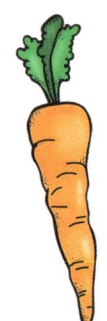    

Say each word and circle the picture that contains the **o** sound.

Which fruit starts with the **g** sound?
Draw a line to match it to the **g**.

Circle two things in the picture that start with the **c** sound.

You cooked up something good there! Draw a smiley face.

ck, e & u

First Try This

Trace the letters below with your pen by following the arrows. Say the sounds as you write them.

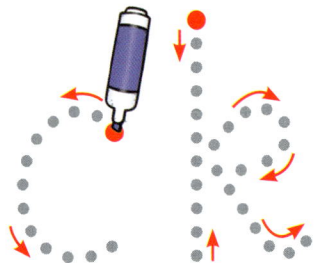 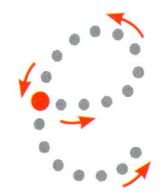 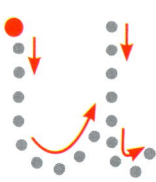

ck makes the same sound as **c** and **k** do on their own. You'll never see **ck** at the start of a word — only the middle or the end.

Now Try These

Put a tick under the picture that starts with the **e** sound.

Circle one thing in the picture that ends with the **ck** sound.

Circle the picture that contains the **u** sound.

Say the words below. Then draw lines to match each picture to the sound you can hear and trace each letter.

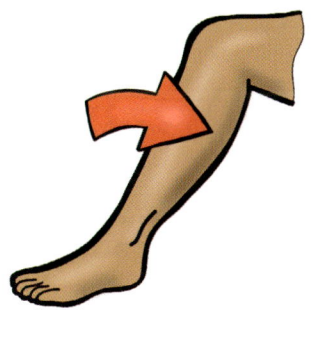  

What is Frankie doing to the ball?
Say the word. Trace the sound you can hear.

    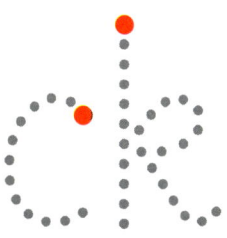

You ran a good race on those pages! Draw a smiley face.

Stepping Stones

Ted is trying to cross the river, but he needs some help. There's an animal guarding each column of stepping stones. Trace the sound at the start of the animal's name. Then draw a line to connect these sounds to show the safe path Ted can take.

You will need sounds from the whole book to do this activity.

Write the letters you have traced on the lines below to find out what Ted finds on the other side of the river, then draw it in the box.

....

r, h & b

First Try This

Trace the letters below with your pen by following the arrows. Say the sounds as you write them.

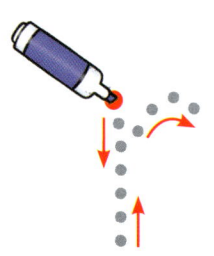 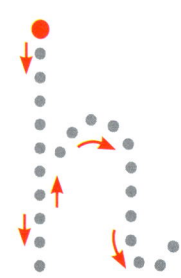 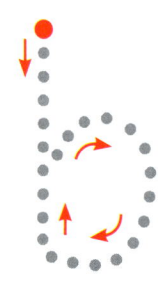 

Now Try These

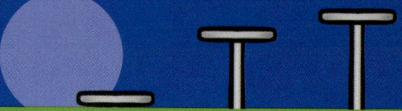

Circle the object on the shelf that starts with the **h** sound.

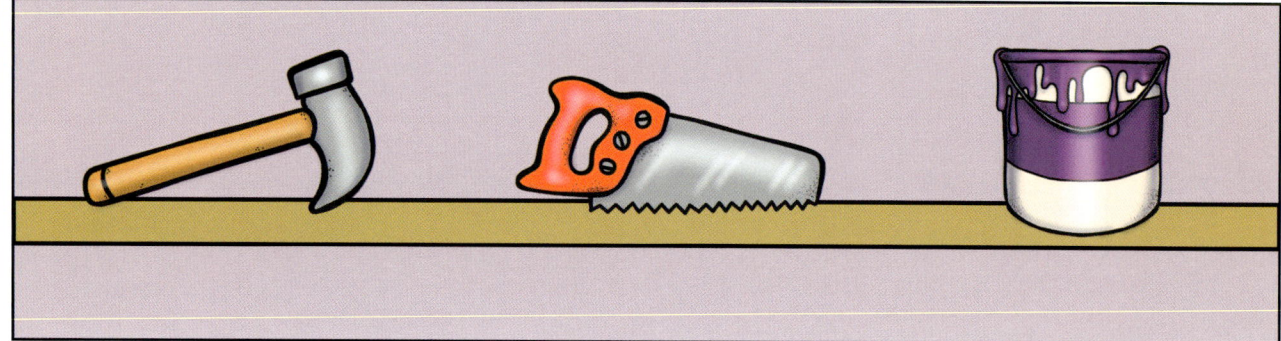

Put a tick under the picture that starts with the **b** sound.

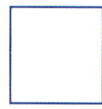 

Trace the letters below.
What colour is each pair of scissors? Draw lines to match each picture to the sound the colour starts with.

Say each word. Circle the picture that contains the **r** sound.

Trace the letters below. Then look at the pictures and circle the sound that both of these words start with.

Well done — you nailed that page! Draw a smiley face.

f, ff, l, ll & ss

First Try This

Follow the arrows with your pen to trace the letters below.

f and **ff** make the same sound.   **l** and **ll** make the same sound.

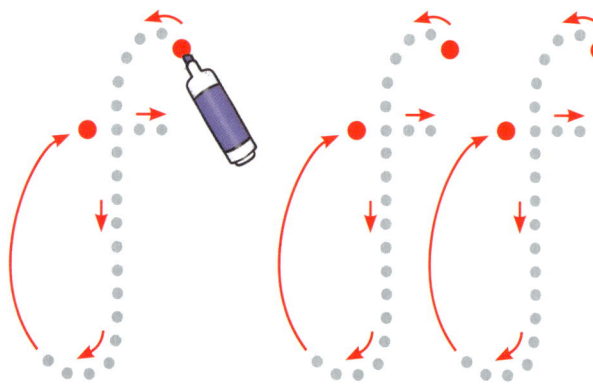

Now practise the **ss** sound.

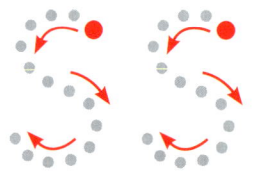

Say the letters as you write them.

Now Try These

Put a tick under the picture that starts with the **f** sound.

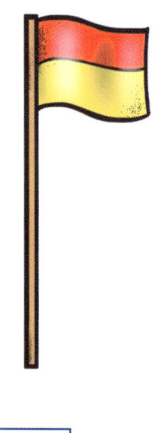  

Circle the picture that starts with the **l** sound.

Trace the letters below.
Then draw lines to match each picture to the sound it contains.

   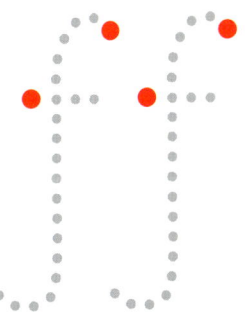

   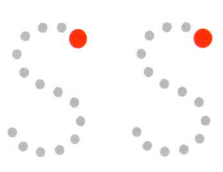

Circle two things in the picture that end with the **ll** sound.

Feeling sunny after that page? Draw a smiley face.

j, v, w & x

First Try This

Trace the letters below by following the arrows with your pen. Say the sounds as you write them.

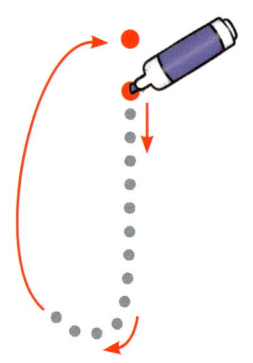 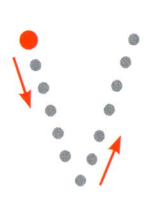 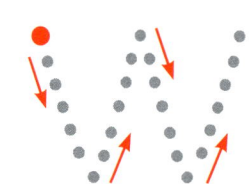 

Now Try These

Put a tick under the picture that starts with the **j** sound.

Which vehicle contains the **v** sound?
Draw a line to match it to the **v**.

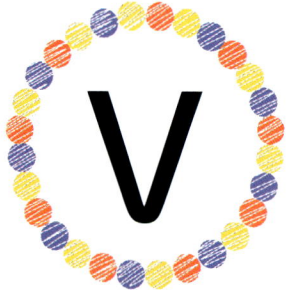

v

What are Jen and Roly doing?
Trace the letter of the sound it starts with.

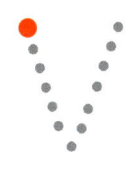

Say each word out loud.
Then circle the vehicle that contains the **x** sound.

Trace the letters below.
Draw lines to match each picture to the sound it contains.

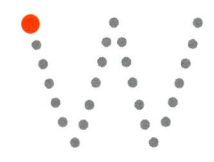

You steered your way through that! Draw a smiley face.

qu, y, z & zz

First Try This

Trace the letters below with your pen by following the arrows. Say the sounds as you write them.

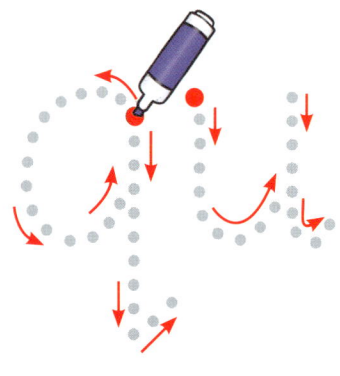 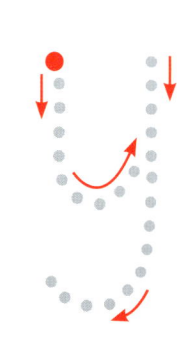  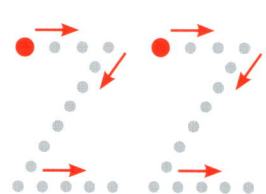

z and **zz** make the same sound.

Now Try These

Circle the picture with the colour that starts with the **y** sound.

Circle the picture that starts with the **z** sound.

What is Jamali telling people to be?
Say the word. Trace the sound you can hear.

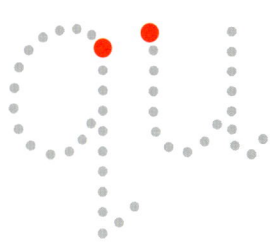

What sound do each of these things make? Say them out loud and find the one that ends in a **zz** sound. Put a tick under it.

 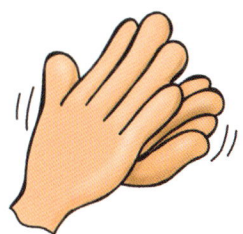 

Lola is feeling tired. What is she doing? Say the word and circle the sound it begins with. Then trace all the letters.

 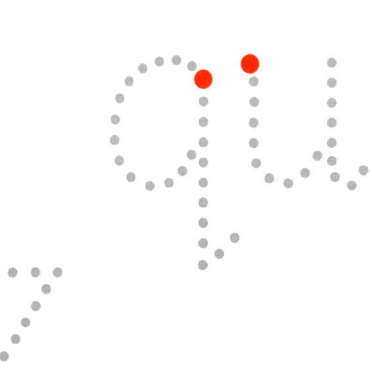

You hit all the right notes there! Draw a smiley face.

Word practice

First Try This

Practise putting sounds together to make words.

Say the letter sounds in the word very carefully.
Then blend the sounds together to say the whole word.
Trace the letters below with your pen.

Now Try These

Trace the missing letters and say each word.
Then draw lines to match each word to the picture it describes.

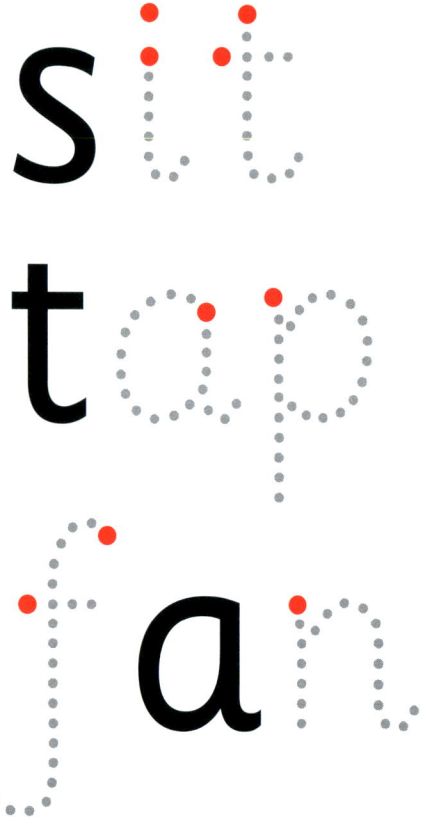

Say the words below.
Draw lines to match each word to the picture it describes.

rug   **bin**   **pot**

Trace the letters and say each word.
Draw lines to match each word to the picture it describes.

You've done it — great job! Draw a smiley face.

Word practice

First Try This

Here are some more words for you to try.
Think about the sounds in each word.
Then trace the letters below with your pen.

s - o - ck  sock

Now Try These

Trace the letters and say each word.
Then draw lines to match the words to the pictures.

 bag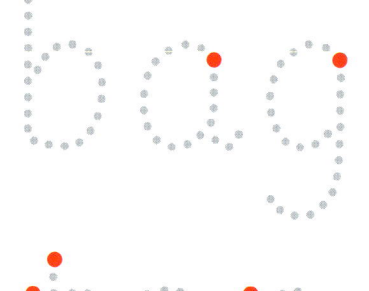

top

 wig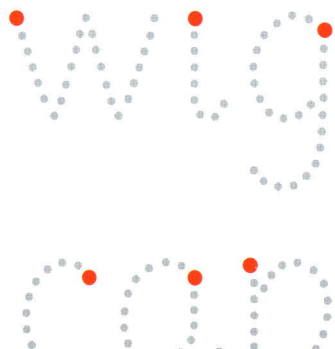

cap

Fantastic word practice! Draw a smiley face.